I and II Thessal(

Jesus Is Coming

*This is a self-study course
designed to help you discover
for yourself, from the Bible,
some important basic truths about
the second coming of Christ.*

how to study the lesson

1. Try to find a quiet spot free from distractions and noise.

2. Read the entire Scripture lesson; read it several times to help you absorb its content.

3. Read each question carefully. Then look up the Scripture reference given after each question. Make sure you have found the correct Scripture passage. For example, sometimes you may find yourself looking up JOHN 1:1 instead of I JOHN 1:1.

4. Answer the question from the appropriate Bible passage. Write, in your own words, a phrase or sentence to answer the question. In questions that can be answered with a "yes" or "no" always give the reason for your answer . . . "Yes, because. . . ."

5. If possible, keep a dictionary handy in order to look up words you don't understand.

1

6. Pray for God's help. You *need* God's help in order to understand what you study in the Bible. Psalm 119:18 would be an appropriate verse for you to take to God in prayer.

7. *Class teachers using this course for group study will find some helpful suggestions on page 47.*

how to
take the self-check tests

Each lesson is concluded with a test designed to help you evaluate what you have learned.

1. Review the lesson carefully in the light of the self-check test questions.

2. If there are any questions in the self-check test you cannot answer, perhaps you have written into your lesson the wrong answer from your Bible. Go over your work carefully to make sure you have filled in the blanks correctly.

3. When you think you are ready to take the self-check test, do so without looking up the answers.

4. Check your answers to the self-check test carefully with the answer key given on page 48.

5. If you have any questions wrong, your answer key will tell you where to find the correct answer in your lesson. Go back and locate the right answers. Learn by your mistakes!

apply
what you have learned
to your own life

In this connection, read carefully James 1:22-25. It is only as you apply your lessons to your own life that you will really grow in grace and increase in the knowledge of God.

Introduction to
The Thessalonian Epistles

Theme of I Thessalonians

1. The Christian and the Lord's return: "Ye turned to God from idols to serve the living and true God, and to wait for his Son from heaven" (1:9, 10). This refers to the time when all believers will be caught up to meet the Lord in the air. This event is sometimes called "the Rapture."

Theme of II Thessalonians

2. "The day of the Lord": "The Lord Jesus shall be revealed from heaven with his mighty angels, in flaming fire taking vengeance on them that know not God. . . . He shall come to be glorified in his saints . . . in that day" (1:7-10). This event should not be confused with the Rapture. The Lord first comes *for* His Church at the Rapture and later comes *with* His Church to establish His 1000 year reign on the earth.

3. Between these two phases of the second coming of Christ is the seventieth "week" of Daniel (DANIEL 9:27), called by the Lord Jesus the "great tribulation" (MATTHEW 24:8, 21).

The writer and two of his companions

4. Does Paul indicate that he wrote these epistles, and that Silvanus and Timotheus (or Timothy) were only co-laborers with him in Thessalonica? (Read the following verses; then answer *Yes* or *No*.)

3

5. By what name is Silvanus called in the following verses?

ACTS 15:22, 27, 32, 40; 16:25, 29; 17:4, 10, 14; 18:5 _____

These passages show that Silas was a Jew, a leader in the Jerusalem church and a companion of Paul on his second missionary journey. ("Silvanus" is the Latin form.)

6. Who joined Paul and Silas at Lystra?

ACTS 16:1-3 _____

7. Evidently Paul had led Timothy to Christ during his first missionary journey. (See ACTS 14:6-23; I TIMOTHY 1:2.) Twelve years later he addressed Timothy as a youth (I TIMOTHY 4:12).

8. Because Silas and Timothy labored with Paul in Thessalonica (ACTS 17:1-10), it was of special interest to the believers there that the apostle included them in his greetings (I THESSALONIANS 1:1; II THESSALONIANS 1:1).

The beginning of the church at Thessalonica

9. How many Sabbath days did Paul teach from the Old Testament in the synagogue at Thessalonica?

ACTS 17:2 _____

10. What did he prove from these "scriptures"?

ACTS 17:3 _____

11. Some of the Jews believed, as well as "a great multitude" of devout Greeks, that is, Gentile proselytes to the Jewish faith (ACTS 17:4). Still others "turned to God from idols" (I THESSALONIANS 1:9). They were evidently Gentiles. This was the beginning of the Thessalonian church.

4

12. Thessalonica was a strategic, commercial city in Macedonia. Many Jews as well as Greeks, Romans and Orientals were included in the population. (You will find the site on the map today, with the modern name, Salonika.)

13. When unbelieving Jews drove the missionaries out of Thessalonica and Berea, to what city did Paul go?

Acts 17:15 _____

14. There he waited for whom to join him?

Acts 17:15, 16 _____

The occasion for the Thessalonian epistles

15. Since Paul could not return to Thessalonica as he so earnestly wanted to do, whom did he send from Athens to establish and comfort the Thessalonian believers?

I Thessalonians 3:1, 2; compare 2:18; 3:10 _____

16. Meanwhile, to what city did Paul go after he left Athens?

Acts 18:1 _____

17. How long did Paul stay in Corinth?

Acts 18:11 _____

18. When Timothy returned to Paul in Corinth, what report did he give of the Thessalonian Christians?

I Thessalonians 3:6 _____

19. Timothy's report led Paul to write I Thessalonians, during his stay in Corinth. It is the earliest of his epistles, written about A.D. 52 or 53.

20. II Thessalonians was written a few months later in Corinth. It has been suggested that when the bearer of I Thessalonians returned with his report, the apostle probably wrote the second epistle.

21. Meanwhile, enemies of Christ and His servant, Paul, had disturbed the Thessalonian church with false doctrine concerning the return of the Lord Jesus, at the same time trying to influence these believers against the apostle. Someone had evidently forged Paul's name to a letter (II THESSALONIANS 2:2) that told the young converts they were in the great tribulation, which will be during that period described by the Old Testament prophets as "the day of the LORD." (See, for example, JOEL 2:1.) In II THESSALONIANS 2:2, "the day of Christ" should be translated "the day of the Lord." "The day of Christ" refers to the Rapture of believers (I CORINTHIANS 1:7, 8; PHILIPPIANS 1:6, 10; 2:16). The "day of Christ" is a time of joy. The "day of the LORD" is a time of judgment. The first has to do with Christ's Rapture of His Church, the second with His rupture of the empire of Antichrist and His own reign on earth.

22. In this course the capitalization in the King James Version is used: "the day of the LORD" (Jehovah) in Old Testament quotations; "the day of the Lord" in quotations from the New Testament.

23. What hope did Paul mention to assure the Thessalonian Christians that they were *not* in the great tribulation?

II THESSALONIANS 2:1 _____

_____

The purpose of the Thessalonian epistles

24. In view of these circumstances, as well as other facts set forth in these two letters, the purpose of the Holy Spirit in guiding Paul to write the Thessalonian epistles is very evident. It was (a) to confirm the young believers in the faith, (b) to exhort them to go on to victory in the face of persecution, and (c) to correct certain errors that had arisen among them, as well as (d) to teach them what God had revealed concerning the Lord's return.

check-up time No. 1

You have just studied some important truths about the background of the Thessalonian epistles. Review your study by rereading the questions and your written answers. If you aren't sure of an answer, reread the Scripture portion given to see if you can find the answer. Then take this test to see how well you understand important truths you have studied.

In the right-hand margin write "True" or "False" after each of the following statements.

1. The Thessalonian epistles were written by Paul, Silvanus, and Timotheus. _____

2. Silas and Silvanus were two different people. _____

3. When in Thessalonica founding the church there, Paul preached in the synagogue on three Sabbath days. _____

4. Like many other ancient cities, Thessalonica is now extinct. _____

5. Hindered from returning to Thessalonica, Paul sent Timothy to help ground and establish the church. _____

6. I and II Thessalonians were the last epistles Paul wrote. _____

7. The "day of Christ" and the "day of the LORD" are the same. _____

8. The Thessalonians were being troubled. _____

9. II Thessalonians was written several years after I Thessalonians. _____

10. The basic theme of I and II Thessalonians is the Lord's return. _____

Turn to page 48 and check your answers.

I Thessalonians
Jesus Is Coming Again!

In view of the Lord's coming, the apostle Paul wrote to the Thessalonian Christians, saying:

> "We give thanks to God for you all . . . remembering without ceasing
>
> > your work of faith . . . ye turned to God from idols
> >
> > your labor of love . . . to serve the living and true God
> >
> > your patience of hope . . . and to wait for his Son from heaven"
>
> > I Thessalonians 1:2, 3, 9, 10

Thanks to God . . . for You All

1:1-10

The greeting   1:1

1. Did Paul, in the opening words of this letter, mention his authority as an apostle?

1:1 _____

2. It was not necessary. To the Thessalonians he wrote as a trusted friend, not needing to defend his apostleship. (Compare I CORINTHIANS 1:1; GALATIANS 1:1.)

3. While Paul wrote this epistle, did he recognize the service of Silas and Timothy in Thessalonica?

1:1 _____

4. For what twofold blessing did the missionaries pray?

1:1 _____

The thanksgiving   1:2-10

5. What words indicate that these servants of God were very definite in their intercession?

1:2 _____

6. How faithfully did they pray for the young converts?

1:3 _____

7. What three spiritual qualities of these believers did the missionaries always remember?

1:3 _____

8. Of what were they very certain?

1:4 _____

Compare I PETER 1:2; ROMANS 8:29.

9. What was one reason for their knowledge of this?

2:13 _____

10. As Paul preached the gospel to the Thessalonians, he was conscious of what power beyond his own words?

1:5; ACTS 1:8 _____

11. When the gospel was first preached in Thessalonica, how was the fury of Satan manifested?

1:6; ACTS 17:5-9 _____

_____

12. Why could these believers endure persecution with joy?

1:6 _____

13. What did their Christlikeness under persecution make them?

1:7 _____

14. The Greek word for "ensamples," literally, "types" or "examples," referred to an instrument for making an impression. From it the English word "type" is derived. The Christians were clearly stamped as true children of God. Their patience under persecution was itself an effective proclamation of the gospel.

15. Why did Paul, Silas and Timothy have no need to tell others of the witness these converts gave to the Lord?

1:8 _____

16. The Greek word for "sounded out" means "a ringing note as of a trumpet," a continuing effect.

17. Note the "three tenses of the Christian life" in 1:9, 10: *conversion*, "Ye turned to God from idols"; *service*, ". . . to *serve* the living and true God"; "the blessed hope," ". . . and to wait for his Son from heaven." The word translated "serve" designates a bond servant.

18. What is the special guarantee of the Lord's return, as He promised?

1:10; Acts 17:31 _____

19. Because He is holy and just, God must judge sin; but because of His love, He offers deliverance from "the wrath to come" (1:10) to all who will receive the Saviour.

check-up time No. 2

You have just studied some important truths about I Thessalonians 1:1-10. Review your study by re-reading the questions and your written answers. If you aren't sure of an answer, reread the Scripture portion given to see if you can find the answer. Then take this test to see how well you understand important truths you have studied.

In the right-hand margin write "True" or "False" after each of the following statements.

1. Paul asserts his apostleship when introducing his letter to the Thessalonians. _____

2. Paul and his companions prayed unceasingly for the Thessalonians. _____

3. Paul says that he could not forget the faith, the generosity and the scholarship of the Thessalonians. _____

4. When Paul preached at Thessalonica, he was very conscious of the Holy Spirit's power. _____

5. The church of Thessalonica was plunged, almost immediately upon its founding, into persecution. _____

6. "Ensamples" means "types" indicating that true Christians bear the divine imprint. _____

7. The Thessalonians had turned to God from idolatry. _____

8. They had become bondslaves of Jesus Christ. _____

9. Paul felt he needed to tell all the people of Macedonia and Achaia about the faith displayed by the Thessalonians. _____

10. The Thessalonians expected Christ to return from heaven. _____

Turn to page 48 and check your answers.

"Put in Trust with the Gospel"

2:1—3:13

1. Evidently the enemies of Christ and His servants had told the Thessalonian Christians that Paul had forsaken them. Therefore, in chapter 2 the apostle makes a strong appeal to correct this falsehood.

Paul's ministry to the Thessalonians   2:1-12

2. Did Paul think his work and that of Silas and Timothy in Thessalonica had been barren of results?

2:1 _____

3. What had they done in Thessalonica after Paul and Silas had been shamefully treated at Philippi?

2:2 _____

4. Who gave these missionaries their boldness?

2:2 _____

5. What three things were missing from Paul's preaching and witness?

2:3 _____

6. What makes preaching or teaching the gospel the highest conceivable responsibility?

2:4 _____

7. What three temptations common to Christian workers had Paul withstood?

a. 2:5a _____

b. 2:5b _____

c. 2:6, 9 _____

8. Paul made tents to earn the money for his temporal needs (Acts 18:3; 20:33-35). As an apostle of Christ, he "might have claimed [the] authority" for his support (2:6, American Standard Version, published in 1901, and indicated in the pages that follow by the abbreviation, A.S.V.).

9. What attitude did Paul and his companions maintain toward the Thessalonian Christians?

2:7 _____

10. Expressing his love for them, Paul continued, "We were well pleased to impart unto you . . . our own souls" (2:8, A.S.V.).

11. What threefold claim did Paul make for his manner of life during his stay in Thessalonica?

2:10 _____

12. He compared himself to what relationship to these believers?

2:11 _____

13. What was Paul's chief concern for the Thessalonians?

2:12 _____

The Thessalonians' faith in the Word of God 2:13-16

14. What effect did the Word of God have in the lives of these persecuted believers?

2:13 _____

15. In apostolic times, what people did most to obstruct the spread of the gospel to both Jews and Gentiles?

2:14-16 _____

16. This opposition was to bring what judgment upon those unbelieving Jews?

2:16 _____

Paul's desire to see the Thessalonians 2:17-20

17. Who had hindered Paul when he had tried twice to return to Thessalonica?

2:18 _____

18. What was Paul's comfort, whether he was permitted to return to Thessalonica or not?

2:19, 20 _____

19. Surely there was great rejoicing in the church at Thessalonica when this letter from their beloved friend was read!

Timothy's return to Thessalonica 3:1-5

20. For what three reasons did Paul send Timothy from Athens to Thessalonica?

3:2, 5 _____

_____

21. Paul was so eager to hear from his persecuted friends that twice he wrote, in effect, "I could no longer forbear" (3:1, 5).

22. What did he consider Timothy able to do?

3:2; II TIMOTHY 4:2 _____

23. During his stay in Thessalonica, what had Paul told the Christians to expect?

3:4 _____

24. Did he expect these Christians to be targets for Satan?

3:5 _____

Timothy's good report to Paul   3:6-10

25. Timothy's "glad tidings" of the Thessalonians' "faith and love" (3:6, A.S.V.) comforted Paul in all his "affliction and distress" (3:7). In 3:8 he wrote, in effect: "Now we can begin to live, since we know you are standing fast."

26. What two proofs of their love must have warmed Paul's heart?

a. 3:6 _____

b. 3:6 _____

27. For what did he give thanks to God?

3:9 _____

28. What was Paul's twofold prayer "night and day"?

3:10 _____

Paul's prayer for the Thessalonians 3:11-13

29. What three petitions are recorded in 3:11-13?

a. 3:11 _____

b. 3:12 _____

c. 3:13 _____

30. Each chapter in I Thessalonians closes with a reference to what future event?

_____

31. Thus the return of Christ for His own is linked with *salvation* (1:9, 10); *service* (2:19, 20); *sanctification* (3:13); *solace* (4: 13-18); *separation* (5:23).

check-up time No. 3

You have just studied some important truths about I Thessalonians 2:1–3:13. Review your study by re-reading the questions and your written answers. If you aren't sure of an answer, reread the Scripture portion given to see if you can find the answer. Then take this test to see how well you understand important truths you have studied.

In the right-hand margin write "True" or "False" after each of the following statements.

1. The persecution of Paul and Silas by the unbelievers at Thessalonica weakened the church's testimony.   _____

2. Guile was what characterized Paul's preaching at Thessalonica.   _____

3. Paul supported himself as a preacher of the gospel.   _____

4. Paul was rough and ready in his presentation of the gospel to the Thessalonians.   _____

5. The Jews were Paul's greatest adversaries on earth as he sought to preach the gospel.   _____

6. Paul had warned the Thessalonians to expect persecution for their faith.   _____

7. The Thessalonian believers sent a message to Paul to say that they wished they could see him again.   _____

8. Paul prayed day and night that he might see them.   _____

9. Each chapter in I Thessalonians closes with a reference to the Lord's resurrection.   _____

10. Paul sent Silas back to Thessalonica to help ground the new church in the things of God.   _____

Turn to page 48 and check your answers.

"Looking for the Blessed Hope"

4:1-18

1. I THESSALONIANS 4:13-18 is one of the clearest Bible passages concerning the Rapture of believers. It is preceded (in 4:1-12) by the apostle's practical exhortation to his fellow Christians for a holy life in view of the return of the Lord Jesus for His own. How they were "to please God" (4:1), even as they were "looking for the blessed hope"—this is the central theme of the chapter. (Read Titus 2:11-13.)

"How ye ought to walk" 4:1-8

2. On whose authority had Paul taught the Thessalonians how they should live as Christians?

4:1, 2 _____

3. "That . . . ye . . . abound more and more" (4:1) speaks of progress in the Christian life.

4. What is "the will of God" for every Christian?

4:3 _____

5. The Bible teaches that sanctification is (a) *redemptive* in that the Holy Spirit sets sinners apart unto salvation (II THESSALONIANS 2:13); (b) *positional* in regard to the believer's standing before God (HEBREWS 10:10); (c) *practical*, the result of constant cleansing by the Word of God (JOHN 17:17; EPHESIANS

5:26). The Christian does *not* get rid of the old, sinful nature in this life; he *is* promised victory over it by the power of the Holy Spirit (Romans 6:1—8:39).

6. In connection with I Thessalonians 4:3-6, read very carefully Romans 6:19; 12:1; I Corinthians 6:13-20; Philippians 1:20.

7. In II Corinthians 4:7 the term "earthen vessels" refers to believers' bodies. Likewise, "vessel" in I Thessalonians 4:4 refers to the Christian's body. Concerning 4:3-6, Charles R. Erdman writes, in part: By the word "vessel" (4:4), does the apostle "refer to one's body or to one's wife? . . . Quite probably he has in mind the holy and reverent regard which a husband should have toward a wife, in contrast with the low and degrading views of marriage so prevalent among the Gentiles. . . .Such pure and honorable marriage should prevent one from invading the sanctity of another's home ('. . . that no man transgress, and wrong his brother in the matter' (4:6, A.S.V.)."[1]

"Love one another . . . and . . . work" 4:9-12

8. How had the Thessalonian Christians already manifested brotherly love?

4:9, 10 _____.

9. What threefold exhortation does the apostle give them in 4:11?

a. _____

b. _____

c. _____

10. Note the word "study." "Avoid religious excitement" (Way translation). Do not be a meddler. Be an efficient worker. Some of the Thessalonians, expecting the immediate return of Christ, were idle, depending on others for their daily bread.

[1]Charles R. Erdman, *The Epistles of Paul to the Thessalonians* (Philadelphia: The Westminster Press, 1935), p. 52.

11. What two reasons are given in 4:12 for the admonition of 4:11?

a. For the testimony before unbelievers _____

_____

b. For the believer's own good _____

The comfort of "the blessed hope" 4:13-18

As you study this paragraph, read all of I Corinthians 15, especially verses 51-57.

12. The Thessalonians were troubled about their Christian loved ones who had died. Possibly they had expected them to live till Christ returned; hence the apostle's comfort in 4:13-18.

13. What fact is the basis for assurance that departed believers are consciously in the presence of the Lord Jesus, and that their spirits will return with Him when He comes at the first resurrection?

4:14; I CORINTHIANS 15:20 _____

14. On whose authority did Paul make these statements?

4:15; JOHN 14:2, 3 _____

15. Who will be first to receive their glorified bodies?

4:15-17 _____

16. When the King James Version was published in 1611, the word "prevent" (4:15) meant "precede."

17. Death to the Christian is not a helpless sinking into a state of unconsciousness until the resurrection (II CORINTHIANS 5:8; PHILIPPIANS 1:23). Rather, in the history of the *body*, it is an in-

cident, a temporary interruption, a step in a process (I Corinthians 15:36).[2]

18. Can there be any doubt that the Lord Jesus Himself will come
bodily and visibly in the clouds of heaven?

4:16; Acts 1:11 _____

19. According to 4:16, what three sounds will be heard by all of
the redeemed?

a. _____

b. _____

c. _____

20. After the unclothed spirits (II Corinthians 5:4) have re-
ceived their glorified bodies, what change will living believers
experience?

4:17 _____

21. "Caught up" is from the word which means "to be seized up
suddenly." It is also used in Acts 8:39 and II Corinthians 12:2.
From the Latin word *rapio*, meaning "to be lifted up," the word
"rapture" is derived, used of the catching away of believers.

22. How quickly will all this take place?

I Corinthians 15:51, 52 _____

[2]"Asleep in Jesus (I Thessalonians 4:14, A.S.V.), as used of departed
Christians, refers to their *bodily* rest. It does not imply total unconsciousness or a state of oblivion.

The Greek has one word for "sleep" which means "to sleep by a power beyond one's self," an administered sleep; and another word for "sleep" which
means "to lie down and sleep by one's choice." The latter is used in
I Thessalonians 5:6 and Matthew 25:5. Both of these words appear in
John 11:11-13. Lazarus had been "put to sleep" in death, but the disciples
understood Jesus to mean that he was merely taking a rest.

The Greek indicates that those who are said to "sleep in Jesus" (4:14)
actually sleep "through Jesus," by His instrumentality. The same word is
found in John 3:17, "through him"; in John 10:9, "by me"; and in John
14:6, "by me." Believers who die are called home to heaven by the direct
will and action of Christ. This is just as definite as His call will be when
He asserts His power in taking them up at His coming.

23. Personal faith in the redemptive work of Christ—not good works or the degree of spiritual attainment—will determine the answer to the question, "Who will be raptured?"

24. What is the most comforting truth for believers whose loved ones have gone "to be with Christ"?

4:13-18; TITUS 2:13 _____

check-up time No. 4

You have just studied some important truths about I Thessalonians 4:1-18. Review your study by rereading the questions and your written answers. If you aren't sure of an answer, reread the Scripture portion given to see if you can find the answer. Then take this test to see how well you understand important truths you have studied.

In the right-hand margin write "True" or "False" after each of the following statements.

1. There is to be progress in the Christian life. _____

2. Sanctification is redemptive, positional, and practical. _____

3. All the brethren of Macedonia had become aware of the brotherly love manifested by the Thessalonian believers. _____

4. In some cases in Thessalonica, expectation of the Lord's near return had led to idleness. _____

5. Our testimony suffers when we are careless about our good behavior. _____

6. It is wrong to believe that departed believers are in the presence of the Lord. _____

7. When a believer dies, he falls into a state of unconsciousness until the resurrection. _____

8. There are grounds for doubting that the Lord's return will be visible and physical. _____

9. At the Rapture, the dead will rise before the living saints are caught up. _____

10. The Rapture will take place in a moment of time. _____

Turn to page 48 and check your answers.

"Watch . . . Rejoice . . . Pray . . . Give Thanks"

5:1-28

Exhortation to "watch and be sober"   5:1-11

1. "The day of the Lord . . . cometh upon them [that is, unbelievers] . . . as a thief in the night" (5:2, 3). "But ye, brethren, are . . . children of light. . . . Therefore . . . watch and be sober" (5:4-6). These two quotations are the key to 5:1-11, the first paragraph of this chapter.

2. What are the main themes of I and II Thessalonians?

a. I Thessalonians 1:9, 10; 4:13-18 _____

b. II Thessalonians 1:7-10 _____

3. When Paul was in Thessalonica, he taught the Christians that God had *not* revealed to man what truth concerning Christ's return?

5:1 _____

Read carefully Matthew 24:36; 25:13; Acts 1:7.

4. While God has not revealed the *time* of the Lord's return, He has given in His Word some definite facts concerning the *order of events* yet to be fulfilled. The following brief summary will help you understand the references to "the day of the Lord" in the Thessalonian epistles:

5. After the Rapture, "the day of the Lord" will run its course. It includes the great tribulation under the rule of the Antichrist, the return of the Lord with His saints, His reign over the millennial earth, and the judgment of all unbelievers at "the great white throne." (See, for example, Joel 2:1; Matthew 24:21; II Thessalonians 2:3; Revelation 13:1-18; 11:15; 19:11-16; 20:11-15.) "The day of God" will follow (II Peter 3:12, 13). It will last forever, and God will be "all in all" (I Corinthians 15:28).

6. After the Rapture, when the unsaved shall say, "Peace and safety," what will come upon them?

5:2, 3 _____

7. The lack of knowledge concerning the *time* of the Lord's return should cultivate what attitude in the believer?

5:4-6; Titus 2:12 _____

8. "Watch and be sober" is, literally, "be wakeful and of sound mind." Watchfulness will prevent indifference to the truth of the Lord's return; a calm spirit will prevent feverish excitement that sometimes leads to fanaticism.

9. Paul urges Christians to put on what armor?

5:7, 8 _____

10. What assurance is given to all believers in Christ that they will go to be with Him at the Rapture, thus escaping the terrible judgments of "the day of the Lord"?

5:9, 10 _____

11. The Greek word used here is translated "hour of trial" and "temptation" in Revelation 3:10 and II Peter 2:9; referring also to the believer's deliverance from the great tribulation.

12. What twofold exhortation is given in 5:11?

13. Toward whom should believers always manifest Christian love and esteem "for their work's sake"?

5:12, 13 _____

14. In verse 14 "unruly" means "disorderly," and "feeblemindedness" is "fainthearted" (A.S.V.). Compare 4:11, 12.

15. How should the Christian spirit always find expression?

5:15 _____

16. In spite of circumstances which may afflict the believer, what "fruit of the Spirit" should ever be seen in his life?

5:16; GALATIANS 5:22 _____

17. "Pray without ceasing" (verse 17) is, literally, "without remission"—giving up.

18. How important is it for the Christian to find something in every situation for which to be thankful?

5:18 _____

19. While the Holy Spirit will never leave the believer in Christ (JOHN 14:16; EPHESIANS 1:13, 14), what can the Christian do to the fires He kindles in the heart?

5:19 _____

20. The word "prophesyings" (5:20) includes all messages prompted by the Holy Spirit. To "prove all things" (5:21) means to distinguish between the true and the false. "Abstain from every form of evil" (5:22, A.S.V.).

Prayer—salutation—benediction 5:23-28

21. What prayer seems to gather all prayers into one?

5:23 _____

_____

22. Note Paul's assurance that God will answer that prayer (5:24).
Note also the warmth of feeling in his personal request for prayer,
salutation and charge that the epistle be read to all the brethren
(5:25-27). As in all of his epistles, the apostle's benediction
(5:28) is a prayer for *grace*—the unmerited favor of God: "The
grace of our Lord Jesus Christ be with you. Amen."

check-up time No. 5

You have just studied some important truths about I Thessalonians 5:1-28. Review your study by rereading the questions and your written answers. If you aren't sure of an answer, reread the Scripture portion given to see if you can find the answer. Then take this test to see how well you understand important truths you have studied.

In the right-hand margin write "True" or "False" after each of the following statements.

1. The day of the LORD will dawn unexpectedly so far as the world is concerned. _____

2. The time of the Lord's coming is revealed in Scripture. _____

3. Man's attempts to produce world peace will be successful. _____

4. The injunction "watch and be sober" is intended to guard against the extremes of indifference and fanaticism in connection with the Lord's return. _____

5. Believers will escape the great tribulation. _____

6. Belief in the Lord's coming is devoid of any practical implications. _____

7. No matter what happens, the true believer should manifest joy. _____

8. God wants the believer to be thankful come what may. _____

9. The believer is to accept without question all that is taught by Bible teachers concerning the Lord's second coming. _____

10. There is real warmth about Paul's concluding remarks in I Thessalonians. _____

Turn to page 48 and check your answers.

II Thessalonians
Jesus Is Coming Again!

In view of the Lord's coming the apostle wrote further to the Thessalonian Christians:

> "To you who are troubled rest with us, when the Lord Jesus shall be revealed from heaven with his mighty angels, in flaming fire taking vengeance on them that know not God . . . when he shall come to be glorified in his saints."
>
> —II THESSALONIANS 1:7-10

"You Who Are Troubled Rest with Us"

1:1-12

1. When Paul wrote his second letter to them, the Thessalonian Christians were still suffering persecution for their faith (1:4). Some were still idle, looking for Christ's immediate return; some continued to be busybodies (3:10, 11). Therefore, Paul wrote (a) to comfort them in their suffering, (b) to teach them more about the return of Christ, especially "the day of the Lord," and (c) to correct disorderly conduct.

Review Lesson 1 for the historical background of the epistle.

The greeting   1:1, 2

2. Who had joined Paul at Corinth?

ACTS 18:5 _____

Thus the apostle names them a second time in his greeting.

3. Paul's greeting includes prayer for what two blessings?

1:2 _____

4. What threefold spiritual growth in the lives of the Thessalonians led Paul to give thanks?

a. 1:3 _____

b. 1:3 _____

c. 1:4 _____

5. The word "bound" (1:3) means to "owe to God as a debt."

6. What blessing is promised these persecuted believers?

1:5 _____

7. "It is a righteous thing" (1:6) for God to act in justice. Remember that He could never be vindictive, for He is holy. Read GALATIANS 6:7.

8. What are the oppressed for Christ's sake bidden to do?

1:7a _____

9. When will this rest (which begins with the Rapture) culminate?

1:7b _____

10. The Greek word for "rest" here is different from that in MATTHEW 11:28. There the reference is to cessation of labor as a means of salvation, rest of heart. The word used here means to "relax," as in the loosening of tension on the strings of a bow. One translation reads: "Find relief with us in the revelation of the Lord Jesus from heaven."

11. According to 1:8, what two charges are laid against those who will meet their doom? (Compare ROMANS 1:28.)

a. _____

b. _____

12. What will be the portion of all who reject Christ?

1:9 _____

13. The Greek word for "destruction" is translated "perdition" in REVELATION 17:8, 11. It does not mean annihilation, as some claim. Compare REVELATION 19:20 with 20:10.

14. In whom will Christ be glorified when He comes again?

1:10 _____

15. "His saints" are "all . . . that believe" (1:10) in Him as their Saviour. He will be glorified in those whom He has made to share in His nature and likeness.

Prayer for the Thessalonians 1:11, 12

16. Paul's prayer can be answered only "with power" from whom?

1:11; ZECHARIAH 4:6 _____

Way translation: ". . . and fulfill your eager aspirations to goodness" (1:11).

17. What worthy motive prompted Paul's prayer?

1:12 _____

18. "That the name of our Lord Jesus may be made all glorious in you" (Rotherham). This prayer could be answered only by "the grace of our God and the Lord Jesus Christ" (1:12).

check-up time No. 6

You have just studied some important truths about II Thessalonians 1:1-12. Review your study by re-reading the questions and your written answers. If you aren't sure of an answer, reread the Scripture portion given to see if you can find the answer. Then take this test to see how well you understand important truths you have studied.

In the right-hand margin write "True" or "False" after each of the following statements.

1. The theme of II Thessalonians is similar to that of I Thessalonians. _____

2. At the time he wrote his second letter to the Thessalonians, Paul had been joined at Corinth by Timothy and Titus. _____

3. Paul felt under a deep obligation to God to give Him thanks for the faith, love and patience of the Thessalonians. _____

4. True relaxation for the Christian begins with the Rapture. _____

5. Failure to obey the gospel brings doom. _____

6. "Destruction" means "annihilation." _____

7. When Christ comes, He will be ashamed of His saints. _____

8. Persecuted believers lose everything. _____

9. Those who do not know God can plead ignorance as an excuse on the day of judgment. _____

10. Paul's prayer in II Thessalonians 1:11, 12 can only be answered in our lives by the power of God. _____

Turn to page 48 and check your answers.

"The Day of the Lord" and "the Man of Sin"

2:1-17

1. Do you have clearly in mind the Bible truths in Lessons 1 and 5 concerning "the day of the Lord"? They are necessary to the understanding of II THESSALONIANS 2. You will remember that "the day of Christ" (2:2) should be translated "the day of the Lord"; and that "the day of Christ" is the Rapture, "our gathering together unto him" (2:1).

"The day of the Lord" is not "present" 2:1-3, 7

2. False teachers had led some of the Thessalonian Christians to fear that, because they were being persecuted, they were in the great tribulation. They were "shaken in mind . . . troubled" (2:2). You will also remember that someone had evidently forged Paul's name to a letter, saying, in effect, "The day of the Lord is just at hand" (2:2, A.S.V.); or, "The day of the Lord is now present."

3. Read 2:1-12, not to consider the details just now, but to find three reasons Paul gives to prove that "the day of the Lord" was *not* then present. (It is still future.)

4. What are these three proofs?

a. 2:3 _____

b. 2:3 _____

c. 2:7 "He who now letteth [restraineth, A.S.V.] will let" ["re-

strain"] until what takes place? _____

_____

5. What evil forces will be at work in the apostasy, "the falling away" from the truth of God's Word?

I Timothy 4:1 _____

Compare II Timothy 3:13; 4:3, 4.

6. The original Greek for "the falling away" (2:3, A.S.V.) is very strong, indicating *the* moving bodily from an original position. The words signify a transferring of the edifice of faith to foundations laid by men. This apostasy is to culminate in man's attempt to exile the God of the Bible and deify in His place the person of "the man of sin."

7. Meanwhile, who is restraining evil in the world?

John 16:7-11 _____

8. What promise of the Lord Jesus to His disciples was fulfilled on the Day of Pentecost?

Acts 1:8; 2:1-4 _____

9. Pentecost marked the birthday of the Church. From that day till the Rapture, the Holy Spirit has worked and will work in and through the Church.

10. To whom does the true Church bear witness by the power of the indwelling Holy Spirit?

Acts 1:8 _____

11. The Church is the body, of which Christ is the Head (Colossians 1:18). When that body is complete and the Church goes to be with the Lord at the Rapture, the restraining power of the Holy Spirit will be removed. Then "the man of sin" will be revealed (2:6-8). "That Wicked" one is more correctly translated "the lawless one" (2:8, A.S.V.).

12. The Holy Spirit will *continue* to work during the great tribulation on behalf of the faithful remnant in Israel and a multitude of Gentiles who will be saved by faith in the Lord Jesus, the Lamb of God. Many will be martyrs for His sake. (See, for example, Revelation 7.)

"The man of sin"   2:3-12

13. When the "man of sin . . . the son of perdition" is revealed, what honor will he demand?

2:4; Revelation 13:4-8 _____

Read Daniel 11:36-39 for other details concerning this "man of sin."

14. "The temple" (2:4) will have been restored in Jerusalem. Compare Daniel 9:27; Matthew 24:15. Note that Paul had told the Thessalonians "these things" while he was with them (2:5).

15. By whose power will this world ruler work "with signs and lying wonders," literally, "wonders of falsehood"?

2:9 _____

16. What judgment will the Lord Jesus execute upon this lawless one?

2:8 _____

17. In 2:8 (A.S.V.) "the spirit of his mouth" is translated "the breath of his mouth" and "destroy" is "bring to nought." The Greek word for "coming" is "presence."

18. What will be the eternal doom of the beast and the false prophet?

REVELATION 19:20; 20:10 _____

19. What are the three downward steps of those who will worship "the man of sin"?

a. 2:10 What will they have rejected? _____

_____

b. 2:11 Therefore, God will send them *judicial* blindness.

What is it called here? _____

c. 2:12 ". . . that they all might be judged" (A.S.V.). *Why?*

_____

Note the order: rejection of the Saviour, strong delusion, judgment.

Paul's thanksgiving—encouragement—prayer
2:13-17

20. In contrast to the unbelief of the apostates, the faith of the Christians in Thessalonica led Paul to thank God for what three proofs of His grace to them?

a. 2:13 What did Paul call them? _____

b. 2:13 Why? _____

_____

c. 2:14 What bliss awaited them? _____

_____

21. The "traditions" of which Paul writes in 2:15 refer to his teaching the gospel (a) orally, "by word"; (b) by his "epistle," that is, I Thessalonians.

22. In view of God's grace to them (2:13, 14), what twofold exhortation does the apostle give in 2:15?

a. _____

b. _____

23. Meditate prayerfully upon every word of Paul's prayer (2:16, 17). What comfort and what challenge it must have brought to the persecuted, troubled Thessalonians! And it is still God's message to Christians today.

check-up time No. 7

You have just studied some important truths about II Thessalonians 2:1-17. Review your study by re-reading the questions and your written answers. If you aren't sure of an answer, reread the Scripture portion given to see if you can find the answer. Then take this test to see how well you understand important truths you have studied.

In the right-hand margin write "True" or "False" after each of the following statements.

1. The expression "the day of Christ" refers to the Rapture.   _____

2. Because they were being persecuted, some Thessalonians thought the great tribulation had come.   _____

3. The "day of the Lord" will be preceded by a worldwide apostasy.   _____

4. The forces of evil are being restrained today by God the Holy Spirit.   _____

5. The Holy Spirit will completely abandon the earth during the great tribulation.   _____

6. "The man of sin," when he appears, will demand that the world worships only him.   _____

7. The rise to power of "the man of sin" will be the simple result of purely natural causes.   _____

8. The Beast (i.e. "the man of sin") will be cast into the bottomless pit when Christ returns in power.   _____

9. Those who reject the gospel lay themselves open to believe the lie.   _____

10. Even in the face of persecution, the true Christian can know real hope and comfort.   _____

Turn to page 48 and check your answers.

"The Lord Direct Your Hearts"

3:1-18

"The Lord direct your hearts into the love of God, and into the patient waiting for Christ" (3:5).

Paul's request for prayer   3:1, 2

1. What two petitions does the apostle mention?

a. 3:1 _____

b. 3:2 _____

2. The first petition is also rendered, ". . . that the word of the Lord may run and be glorified" (A.S.V.). Compare Psalm 147:15. Paul desired God's Word to speed along like a swift messenger. In the second petition he probably had in mind the enemies of Christ in Corinth (ACTS 18).

3. How does Paul express his approval of the Thessalonians for having "glorified . . . the word of the Lord"?

3:1 _____

Paul's confidence in the Lord   3:3-5

4. Paul trusted the faithfulness of the Lord for what twofold spiritual growth in the lives of the Thessalonians?

a. 3:3 _____

b. 3:3 _____

5. In whom did the apostle place his confidence for their obedience to his commands that follow in 3:6-15?

3:4 _____

6. Paul's prayer in 3:5 is for what two petitions?

a. _____

b. _____

The last phrase is "the patience of Christ" (A.S.V.).

Instruction concerning the disorderly   3:6-15

7. What attitude were the obedient believers to take toward the disorderly—the idlers and busybodies?

3:6, 14 _____

8. Being "disorderly" means to "break ranks" from the "tradition" —Paul's oral teaching when he was in Thessalonica.

9. What high purpose was to prompt such a course?

3:14 _____

10. What exhortation to Christian love did Paul add?

3:15 _____

11. What command had Paul given the Thessalonians when he was with them?

3:10 _____

12. What command and exhortation did he now give?

3:12 _____

13. How had Paul's conduct in Thessalonica been an example in these things?

a. 3:7 _____

b. 3:8 _____

14. Compare Acts 18:3; 20:34. "Follow us" (3:7, 9) is rendered "imitate us" (A.S.V.).

15. What two reasons did Paul give for thus earning his daily bread?

a. 3:8 _____

b. 3:9 _____

16. Compare "not because we have not the right" (3:9, A.S.V.) with I Thessalonians 2:6; I Corinthians 9:12-14.

17. What encouragement does the apostle give to those who had been obedient in these things?

3:13; Galatians 6:9 _____

Prayer—salutation—benediction   3:16-18

18. Paul's prayer, his salutation in his own handwriting, and his own characteristic benediction close the epistle. "Peace" and "grace" from "our Lord Jesus Christ" and His abiding presence are gifts from Him to all who love Him.

check-up time No. 8

You have just studied some important truths about II Thessalonians 3:1-18. Review your study by re-reading the questions and your written answers. If you aren't sure of an answer, reread the Scripture portion given to see if you can find the answer. Then take this test to see how well you understand important truths you have studied.

In the right-hand margin write "True" or "False" after each of the following statements.

1. Paul was very zealous for the spread of God's Word. _____

2. It is permissible for the Christian to pray to be delivered from unreasonable and wicked people. _____

3. Our being established in the faith and being kept from evil depends absolutely upon ourselves. _____

4. It is contrary to Christian love to have nothing to do with idlers and busybodies. _____

5. Those under church discipline are to be counted as enemies by other Christians. _____

6. If a man will not work he should not eat. _____

7. Paul's own conduct when at Thessalonica had been exemplary. _____

8. Paul wanted the Thessalonians to imitate him. _____

9. It is possible to get tired of doing good. _____

10. Paul signed II Thessalonians himself. _____

Turn to page 48 and check your answers.

Suggestions for class use

1. The class teacher may wish to tear this page from each workbook as the answer key is on the reverse side.

2. The teacher should study the lesson first, filling in the blanks in the workbook. He should be prepared to give help to the class on some of the harder places in the lesson. He should also take the self-check tests himself, check his answers with the answer key and look up any question answered incorrectly.

3. Class sessions can be supplemented by the teacher's giving a talk or leading a discussion on the subject to be studied. The class could then fill in the workbook together as a group, in teams, or individually. If so desired by the teacher, however, this could be done at home. The self-check tests can be done as homework by the class.

4. The self-check tests can be corrected at the beginning of each class session. A brief discussion of the answers can serve as review for the previous lesson.

5. The teacher should motivate and encourage his students. Some public recognition might well be given to class members who successfully complete this course.

answer key
to self-check tests

Be sure to look up any questions you answered incorrectly.

Q gives the number of the test *question*.

A gives the correct *answer*.

R refers you back to the place in the lesson itself where the correct answer is to be found.

Mark with an "x" your wrong answers.

TEST 1			TEST 2			TEST 3			TEST 4		
Q	A	R	Q	A	R	Q	A	R	Q	A	R
1	F	4	1	F	1	1	F	3	1	T	3
2	F	5	2	T	6	2	F	5	2	T	5
3	T	9	3	F	7	3	T	8	3	T	8
4	F	12	4	T	10	4	F	9	4	T	10
5	T	15	5	T	11	5	T	15	5	T	11
6	F	19	6	T	14	6	T	23	6	F	13
7	F	21	7	T	17	7	T	26	7	F	17
8	T	21	8	T	17	8	T	28	8	F	18
9	F	20	9	F	15	9	F	30	9	T	20
10	T	24	10	T	17	10	F	20	10	T	22

TEST 5			TEST 6			TEST 7			TEST 8		
Q	A	R	Q	A	R	Q	A	R	Q	A	R
1	T	1	1	T	1	1	T	1	1	T	1
2	F	3	2	F	2	2	T	2	2	T	1
3	F	6	3	T	4	3	T	4	3	F	5
4	T	8	4	T	10	4	T	4	4	F	7
5	T	10	5	T	11	5	F	12	5	F	10
6	F	12	6	F	13	6	T	13	6	T	11
7	T	16	7	F	15	7	F	15	7	T	13
8	T	18	8	F	6	8	F	18	8	T	14
9	F	20	9	F	11	9	T	19	9	T	17
10	T	22	10	T	16	10	T	23	10	T	18

how well
did
you do?

0-1 wrong answers—excellent work

2-3 wrong answers—review errors carefully

4 or more wrong answers—restudy the lesson before going on to the next one